The Pact

Also by Jennifer Militello

Poetry

A Camouflage of Specimens and Garments
Body Thesaurus
Flinch of Song
Anchor Chain, Open Sail

Nonfiction

Knock Wood

The Pact

Jennifer
Militello

Tupelo Press
North Adams, MA

Library of Congress Control Number: 2020950317
ISBN-13: 978-1-946482-47-1

Cover and text design by Bill Kuch. Composed in New Caledonia and Mona Lisa solid ITC TC.

First paperback edition May 2021

Tupelo Press
P.O. Box 1767
North Adams, Massachusetts 01247
(413) 664-9611 / Fax: (413) 664-9711
editor@tupelopress.org / www.tupelopress.org

Tupelo Press is an award-winning independent literary press that publishes fine fiction, non-fiction, and poetry in books that are a joy to hold as well as read. Tupelo Press is a registered 501(c)(3) non-profit organization, and we rely on public support to carry out our mission of publishing extraordinary work that may be outside the realm of the large commercial publishers. Financial donations are welcome and are tax deductible.

ART WORKS.
arts.gov

This project is supported in part by an award from the National Endowment for the Arts.

For TL

Contents

Love is all you need.

—The Beatles

Agape Feast

What is love but the bruise or the abrasion,
the fruitlessness, the deep incision. What
is love if it isn't on stage or placed
between two sonnets' turns. What is love
nerving down the spine. Just now I thought
I felt it stir, or heard it, like the wall's
small nest of baby mice. Like chemicals
set to preserve imported furs. Its complaint
got in, rain astringent at its end.
Fat as a blackberry, thin as a stick,
stationed overseas at the vein-itch
or artery-strap. Bubble, flutter of pain.
An emptiness pinned to its lapel.
It is an aftermath at best. *Shhh* is
what it says. *Dear, diagram yourself.*
Its pigeons shuttle like the imbalance
of a hat. Pores seen. Lips curled.
It is not the documents correct. Stamps
are streaked away with bleach. Bags
are searched. The fingers of government
workers black with ink. Its ribs
grate like gnashed teeth. It sings like
the polished floors of a bank. It reads
all the lines in your palm as the equivalent
of death. Carrier of diseases and lice,
wool blanket stink. Fire beneath the bridge.
Its past is a chasm. Its past is a lid. Let it
catch at the latch of your throat and body bag
your want and infinity your need. Its Jesus
is the noose at your neck. Its Jesus is
the blue slits veins seem at your wrist.
Its mercy is electric, it is storied, it is rank.
Its mercy is a tablet dissolved in a glass,
more invisible the more you drink.

Species

We come from three generations of gunsmiths
and armorers. Our pride name is Swahili for dust.
We sew necklaces together from doorknobs

and knucklebones and eye sockets and teeth.
We weep at the sight of sugar cane cut.
Our headlamps reveal the skull of a jaguar,

precise stone men, staircases hollowed, a two-edged
knife. Sacrifices seem another form of astronomy.
Pyramids predict the face of the earth. Our gardens

grow fructose. Our hands fill with cake. We emulate
the rasps of frogs. What we eat is processed in the liver.
Legally hunted lions hang, wilted to bone.

We poison livestock. We rescue rafts. We patrol borders
marked by marooned populations. Our spines
are the spokes of motorcycle wheels. Our longships

empty. Our rodents stow. Our goldenrod produce toxin.
Our gallflies perch. Our offspring hatch. Our onslaughts
happen. Our coral reefs pulse. We exit through fences

we then repair. We survive the dry season. We crave meat.
Our dark manes correlate with robustness. Our Asian carp
are tenacious. Our wildebeest rank high as prey.

Lineage Is Its Own Religion

I was an apostle to the group of you, strangers
who had known me since I was born. I ate
of your flesh. I drank of your blood. Sipped
the elixir of your moods. Put the remainders
in the tabernacle, wiped the goblet clean with
a cloth. The crosses branded into the wafers
were your voices branded onto my heart.
I heard you live forever. I heard you rise.
The bones of you yield to the memory of flesh,
and we count our blessings and also bless.
We are bright in anticipation of death,
we are living like fissures and set against waste,
and the taste is bitter, left in our mouths.
I am dying, I am dead, lord of the losses, lord
of the faith. I take each breath and my chest
expands. Now I stand knee deep in the muck
unable to move, and if I dip my hands in,
they will fill with bracken and all the thickness
of each formless face, kicking up stones,
until you are gone, mythic lisp the lips
shape. One day, you vanish like a flash.
Confessions in a dark room. Firmaments to read
and spin like dice. I genuflect twice at the edge
of your pews. I kiss the book for you. This is what
the word of family can do. Sit at the round table.
Break bread. In the beginning, the loveless
made the world and saw that it was good.

Jennifer Militello

Sibling Medusa

In the pictures, the hair snakes all look the same,
though I know better. Every snake is a different
persona, though all are out for murder.

Every hiss is a criticism unfettered. Every
head is a hatred on its leash. Every slither is
a movement toward hurting me further

like our mother. I learned long ago to only
approach you from the mirror. Your scales
overlap; they have the phalanx of your heart.

All my shields crumble, all my winged shoes fail.
You are my sister. My love for you is a ladder
I climb until I fall. There is a Red Sea in my blood

and it is your mood, venomous at root, ever-changing
as a god. There is a Red Sea in my blood and
I must keep it still as its tides would drown us,

as our parents still hope we will break bread.
We believed you were a priestess. We put you
on the urns, we lifted you up and loved you alone.

Now you are a monster and want me gone. Were I
to carry it as a weapon, your head would turn on me.
I am only one of the statues that surround your lair.

All of our family is there, posed and still, paralyzed
by your punishment, your scathe, your skill.
Where I had my home, I am no longer at home.

I was closest. I was in your crib. I was in your bed.
I wore your clothes. I shared your name. Is this
why you hate me? Is this why I now see the deadly

inside red of a thousand stretched-open mouths?
Your serpents control me. Your eyes are voiced over.
I don't know you. Where is my sister.

Sibling Invention

Now we invent you from a cotton swab
and unclean syringe. Now we draw
the curtains. Nurses visit. Excuses drop
like fruit. What you thought was

the presence of water was a shadow.
What you thought was heaven is an ice cap.
Each eye the hatching of a reptile, your chin
happening in waves. Thin as paper dolls,

your eyelids clamp. Hairline a reason
to weep or a misplaced wisp of light.
How the fingers flex and grow precise.
How the fingers ignite. Elbows jointed

with replacement hips. Metal fittings. Socket
and ball. Femurs and jawbones arranged.
A microscope making visible cells inside
the cheek. You of the placid, of gas,

liquid, or solid, the Novocaine tract. Float
to the bottom of a lake, be a mythological
monster none will believe. Now we see you,
hysterical, and with enough stimuli

to shatter your balance and accelerate
a heart. Now we see you like
a peppered moth darkening from the markings
of the past. Now your overflow is a form

of fashion. Now there is surely
an animal rotting in the air ducts,
now there is warm milk, rock you
to sleep. Now you spill over coincidence

into intent. Your anger is a dream
we wake from, having chipped the edges
of our teeth. Your anger is a tiled floor
gapped and cracking, asbestos underneath.

Sibling Bipolar

Quiet. Quiet. I diet on your wounds.
I blizzard on your hum. Your underdog
or din. I satin on your fur. Lithium
on your purr. What is it to lose
or win. You are the layers behind
my grimace. You are the cough that
clears my lung, the car I second gear,
the clutch I release, the rant
I clutch, grease I layer, layer I latch.
You are my match, lit with rain.
My water stain, ceiling sag, my stalactite,
my bottled gin, you are the lisp I fin
from lips too still to speak or sing.
I was ragged, sister. I was drugged.
I was alert for you. I understand
now the villain I am. Kithing had
a Satan to it. A suicide. A rust. The drag
of God burning like pollen, the drag
of mummification in the psyche
like a stench. I fell, but how far.
I botched the pretty maids all in a row.
My own hands disobeyed me in a disco
up to par. No one can recognize
the glitter or ribbon or wrench.
No one. Warming our hands at kin
we will not touch. We jewel what earthworms
like a blouse. I mint a limit to you.
Here is a liquid. Here is a cliff. I have
never been a child as far as I can tell.
I will tremor shut the ending in its box.
You will leap at the chance, awake. In the daze
of adoration, I go mute. There is no tune I
sing to. I go cruel. Or acute. Where is the handbook
for the embellishment of you. Could I quell

the empire you rule, what names I could
redo. What I have done ticks like a bomb.
I explode from under it, painkiller dream.
Reams of it reign. I dare to steer. I dare to
stretch. I dare to blame the fidget,
the flinch. I can't get inside the tattoo
you assembled to protect you. I can't get
inside that amnesiac November to test
the quill of a leaf. Radio me here,
at the frequency or botch. Frequency
of zone or zilch. Film me as I dwindle.
Spot me as I launch.

Sibling Frankenstein

When you take its pulse, the dead cell lurches.
The dead cell does not lurch. It opens with

a gasp like a pressurized safe or a glacier
calving from itself, blinks ajar like a mudslide

and expels. Fills with phosphorus and singes
flesh. A little revenge. It wants to be dead.

When you hook up electricity and let it spike,
she rises hooded like a cobra, oh nucleus, she

rises microbial as a mouth. It happens aloud,
this snap like a cry: you can wake her after all.

Her insides shudder and her borders quake.
She will swallow particles. She will digest.

Her returning will graft like rain. Lids thinned
to mesh. Crow sounds graveling like pebbles

in a fist. Her anatomy strung from cultured
snarls. Bedded down in a wither of cork.

But the brink in her hiss indicates she is
not fixable. She is endeavoring to sever you.

It will always be like this. She was a dime
until spent, a rhyme scratched in ink. Organs

pumped and shadowed, organs baked of clay.
She and her machine dislike you. She will

have you on your knees, cowering at noise.
Enough, you say. Pronounce the living girl a corpse.

Sibling Parasitic

Larva, wake up. You are the vermin
that sat at the wicker basket of me and
tried to suggest rot. You are the worm
the summer hues asked of me, hatching in
a cup. You with only the length of a curl,
not the kind a cat vomits up, not
the kind to damage the heart. Not
the kind to seem a scratch then manage
to feed at the skin like lice. When I see
you, some old me hurts. The me that
has an ancestral haunt. The body a comma.
The body a scald. A bit of twine one
cannot trim up. What will you gestate
into if I wait? Days pool like gone-bad
meat. I wear the ankle bracelet you
request of me. On house arrest, I fester
like mistake. Your grotesque aging
like the hang of blood. What is this
cocooning of my mood. What am I
if I cannot grow wings. How dare you
try to hazard me, watch and thrash
like a severed tongue or line at the palm
of a hand. Like a seam or vein drawn
in sand. I get beyond the place
where I can imagine you as anything
more than your maggot self. You
will not end. I leave you where
you make many more. So help you.
The goddess world flirts with these
ornate versions of you, scabs over like
a sin, in the char is singed new, is singed
real. The weak line up and are eaten.
The dominant reproduce. This
continent has yet to bloom. Its desert
is a boot heel. Its desert is a thumb.

Jennifer Militello

Ode to Superstition

Their swamp gas stars us with axe marks,
their frictions affix us with dust.
Their legions float the orphans in us

like fetus-jarred oblivions. They embroider
our skin with the demons it deserves,
they henna our falsehoods with the beauty

of a slap. They priest our sins into place.
All the superstitions celebrate their venom,
their hoofprints work in stone or wood,

their rattles fabricate at the ends of their tails.
All the sketches of them monsters, all
the herds of them earth. All the superstitions

whiten like a worm on a hook. Their bodies
lengthen in rain, shrink in the sun.
No to the swans of their necks, no to

their nail-bitten weather, no to their whiskey
neat in the glass. Drink them down
and they smoke in the throat. Layers

peel. Names sip. No to their intricate silence.
No to their breathless downpour sweep.
The way they know you inside out.

The way their statues grackle stiff.
The way their faces crack like teeth.
Who can kneel at such a cross. Who

can count on such chickens to hatch.
Who can scratch at the edges, or
mark such bedposts with even a notch.

Homesickness Is a Geographic Nostalgia

Home: it is the undergrowth in me
that grows over, that tangles and
takes cover and is awake and cannot
be staked down. It is the vine
or brush that will not be burned
or groomed or cured or curled,
at its bracket or martyr or marrow,
at its emptiness minus branches,
an answer or a bruise. This poverty

in me you mistake for sleep. This cape
I wear as if to cope. This open door
like a sore healed over or a shape
one may shift. This part of me
adrift or lost at sea. This part of me
the blight one cannot cure. This
part of me unsure and bearing witness.
If I am a story, this is the caesura.
If I am a cello, this is its string.

Home has an ownership of me I milk
or battle. Home has in me a rattle
I make of the way light falls, voice
another breathes. I grieve its likeness
like a lover. I grieve it now that it is
over. I dig for it like gold. I bury it
in the ground. Store the fat. Salt
the meat. Understand the starve to come
until it blooms like moths. Not one

sound mimics its hover. I feel for it
and its smother, its smock, its collar,
its wool coat, its clover, all I am
when with another, all I am when

Jennifer Militello

also alone. Its wolf tone or soured liver.
Its hospice or clouded mirror. Its
ribbon, rack, or battered father. If it is
a beaker, I am the experiment. If it is
the bubble, I am the reaction. If it is
the laboratory, I am ready to explode.

Oxymoronic Love

Hatred is the new love. Rage is right. Touch
is touch. The collars of the coat, turned down,
point up. The corners of our hearts are smoothed
with rough. Our glass breaks slick, our teeth
rip soft. The mollusk of me, shell-less.
If the future once was, the past predicted
us. The street gives off rhythm. The sun
gives off dusk. When we walk, we
pour backward. When we have nothing,
it's enough. The hunger leaves us satisfied,
the fullness leaves us wrung. The sum of all
its parts is whole, the reap of it has roots, not
took or plucked. Far apart, we move inside
our clothes: open is old, young is closed. The fangs
we used to bare are milk teeth grown from gums.
The fire we used to be scathed by numbs. We
run on the track of our consumption, done.
We've been ice when liquid is our natural state. .
We've worn our husks, we've clenched our fists.
We scold and punish, scrape, pay a price.
We dole out in slanders what has no weight.
We pay in cringing for the moments. We open
injuries in one another. We lacerate places
that flex like knuckles, crack and grow. We are
sipping from the water's thirst. We were lost
at first. From the finish, begun. We undergo
pain the other knows. We are cartoon yards
where dogs dig for lost bones. Esoteric,
we are full of holes. That need to be filled.
That need to be dug. We are under-loved.
We are under-known. Give to us and we are
downcast and uplifted and sift like water
and sand like stone. We are greedy, we are
gone. We are helpless, we are prone. Drain us

or fill us and we'll ache a vast installment.
Let us empty. Let us alone. Madness
is our happiness. Sadness is our home.

&

Darling, you are my boxed-in place, my razor blade,
my vinegar state. We aim for crazed, we go

to waste. Darling, together we tether and take.
Nightly, I am the game you plate, the scorched-raw

meat, too tart for taste. We sip and savor,
simmer and baste. We lick the spoon,

we boil the trace. Clean-strip the bones, permit
their grace. I creep and creep. I crawl and pray.

How little can a poor girl take? You hemorrhage
my breath, you leech my ache. You vampire me,

estrange, my freight. You ravaged average. Bloody break.
You then engender my disgrace. Darling, you are the neck

I brace: we hit the wall, we slam the brakes. You are
the maw, the clamp, the rake. Bootlace, foothold,

briefcase, bass. I claw the windows, claw the grate.
You snap the whip and clasp the gate. I want it now,

the great escape. My own Houdini, chains
tensed straight, doors torn open: I cradle and drape.

I want to lapse, to rage and wake. Real me now til I am fake.
Hold me now until I quake. God, this hour, moth-eaten

stain, this ringlet shell, this deadly strain. My windpipe
is your souvenir, my heart a stone, a sealed keepsake.

Chemistry

Don't fuse, at least. Don't beaker. Don't
measurement or Bunsen burner. Don't escalate
or eat at liver. The liver will grow back.

Don't dinner with a starter. Ask for me
or meet my father. Don't mix chemicals
or bring me flowers. Don't expect

electrons to migrate rings. Don't sing
or seem to bother. Don't adamant
or collar. Don't let adolescence

barter with what you want or what
you need. Don't burn to see its color,
pattern inner models, flame to show

a hover. Darwin anything but lean.
Don't mix to see what bubbles up
or hex to see what tremors south

or water to see what implodes suddenly
or catalyst to maximize or aim.
Don't find a groove. The elements

would disapprove. Their very numbers,
their very ooze. Things match or
glance, wish, invent, or take to task,

march like the worst of accidents.
Flinch: don't change. Don't let day
make of you a puppet. God is a glitch

in time, and is significant. And tired.
Don't mix what can't be stable. Don't
incorrectly label. Don't let the spill

of things wish ill on the remaining air.
Don't kneel among the sheer you
shiver. As if fingers would snap,

tipped with glitter. It could
eat you, then could keep you.
Is not a firefly jars would hold.

Anubis Love

You: the color of clay.
Naked as a vase, with curves
soft and square at once. Voice
a parchment, its dust wraps and
gem stones embedded in the breast,
in the dark cave of the rib cage,
in the turban of the chest. Hands
like linen strips, hieroglyphs, spider
through their maze of sun-baked bricks.
Our organs know their forms of preservation,
our organs have their canopic place.

Weigh my heart against a clock, a seed;
eternity will tip the scales. Our shabti slaves
row amulets to dreams until we find
their water in the air. The ear has its lobe,
the nose has its ring, the brain
has a zipper we must not unlace.
The lip has a sing to it, a whisper
of wine or alabaster far from the grave.
In their air-tight chamber, brush of natron,
dip of amber, desiccation sintering to glaze.

Geographic Tongue

Curled, it bristles like the back of a cat. Quiet,
it makes a backbone of a ditch. Dorsal migrations,
textured tufts. Rivulets that undulate. Addled
slopes. Its root flattens. Its apex folds. It moistens

your finger as you flip a page. It radiates,
pronounces words. *Tunge* or *tonge, tunga, zunge.*
It cleans your fur, it grooms your pelt,
removes parasites or regulates heat.

It sweats like skin to cool your mouth. It
catches prey. Prehensile. Disarranged. It has been
your opposable thumb. It has been your jointed bone.
Its atrophy of papillae. Its scalded feel. Split, it licks

the air, sips nectar, laps and pants. It widens and
narrows, softens and withdraws, wets your lips, flicks out,
flicks in. It is silver, it is forked, it tells lies and reinvents
them as truth. It tells me what I want to hear. It rallies

a world that isn't real. It rebuilds my city, it alters
my name. It makes for me a padded solitude, a hologram
in which to live, a swimming pool beside which
to cool. To dip my hands toward, be reflected in. What

you tell me snakes through its canyon walls, echoes
and bends, slips through androgen cracks, grows elastic,
comes awake. What you say takes on a life mapped
by variations and sprung traps, and what emerges

settles out like sand in the palm, some gone through
the fingers like bread on a trail, like children lost.
Syllables crimp and craw and the edges of utterances trim
and compress. Moving through the gut of it, digested

from one form to another, expelled. All you have been
is knitted there, in its many-sided, meticulous buds,
its lisps and ties, sweet back and sour tip.
Our mother tongue. You speak in it.

Odaxelagnia

When I sink my teeth into you,
there is a taste, a satisfaction, the start
of a match, the catch in your throat.
We are rich with the exhilarations
of our blood, we are rich with our
print-blackened roots, like the crowns
of my canines in you cracked like dirt,
enamel-fragile and eggshell-veined. I sink
my teeth and they knit your history
a coat. I shut the cold like a tap
and lean like a trunk and we unravel
as though thread and when we fall,
the quiet is like a feather, like
a bough. It was a God I held
in the trap of my mouth, in you,
my rabbit gone limp, my bite
at your neck and me tasting fur
like wind and me tasting the scent
of you melted as wax. A wick lit,
it was my path, it was a desire
to solidify and start. At the front.
At the back. In the lip. At its cry.
No dry soul unsickened yet. I sink
my teeth. I notch your depth. I prove
it has terror, an Atlantic I've wept.

Erotomania

Do not asphyxiate the bitch in me.
Do not turn and nude your teeth.
Do not minx the honeybee. Do not
develop or serenade the w(he)e.

You is to hydration as blood is to bleed.
You is to system as single is to me.
Do not slot your throat. Don't sugar
your greed. All the antibodies antidote, debris.

Do not irk or plead or please. Do not
frivolous the cylindrical in me. I am away.
As I am here. Do not glare the temporal,
the seize. Do not com-pair me with my

arteries. When the result is tissue injury. When
the result is climate change. I have a mileage
up in flames. The temperatured cells.
The spatial ear. You come closer to hearing

what I sign, you come closer to being
what I fear. I do not dare to gloam beneath
the dare. I am circulatory, I am here.
The scabies of the wrist. The saline

of the bite. Long bones ignite. In
the marrow cavities, our needs are met.
Sinuses dense the naked eye. Muscle fibers
thicken to fittings and cogs. Reflexes

are dogged. Sensory branches synapse
with light. Do not apply pressure too soon
or the membrane stitches, or the name glitches,
or the appendage hitches, or the none of us bloom.

Jennifer Militello

Pledge

I promise I will know you like the back of a hand,
like the sound of a slap. I promise I will know you
like the ways I react. I promise to let you

brainwash me. I swear I will be tortured, let
droplets pelt my head. I will let you electrify me
and jolt me dead. I will let my lucidity go adrift.

I will shed everything I love. Pack my belongings.
Throw out the cat. Cage the hens. Let the roaches
starve. Let the hinges on the red fence rust. I promise

I will lie for you. I promise I will let you lie back.
I will frequent basements, damp closets, the always-wet
area of the carpet just under the well pump to remember

our mildew-scented bed. I promise my clothes will
smell of it next. I promise to be gripped. I promise
to eat too slowly. I promise to forget who you are.

I promise to drink too fast. I promise to hit
the target. I promise to take the bait. I promise
to accept the guilt. I promise to confess. I swear

I will watch hail spell our names in dirt. I will
brush dogwood petals from the back of your coat.
I will become illegal. I will give up control.

I promise you tax evasion. I promise you fraud.
I offer you suffocation. I offer you an overdose.
I promise to submit. I will rob a bank. I will recruit.

I will walk you to slaughter while saving your life.
I will sneak past the guard, climb a barbed wire fence.
I will snap out of the trance, resist hypnosis,

wake. I will drag you from your bed. Against
your will, I promise to find you. I will introduce
objects from your past. I will make of us plaster statues,

capture our faces, cast our limbs. I will skim the surfaces
of us with the mind's clear milk and mold us to a shape.
I will place us inside a half-filled glass. I will let us

overflow the surface. I will nurture you and hurt you.
I will make you plain. I will sand you smooth. I will
marvel at you. I will make of you a paper skear.

I will speak in languages you never learned. I will
write your obituary. I will read your palm. I will not
martyr entrances for the exits they become.

Fretwork

What comes moors itself like a claw or core.
A child's shoe built into a wall, dressmaker's dummy
mute and white among the trees. What comes
knuckles sulfur and ulcers our remains.
What comes combs at me and at my body.
Wants more. Gives less. Its edges knock.
It has medicine that almost masks a cure.

I should be more concerned, I know. It goes
leaking its dark fluid. It goes mistaking me
for who I am. It goes for broke, but thinks to succeed
as a grimoire or prayer. It spits and stretches
its root-like limbs. It crouches like a collarbone
in its god-like niche. The caverns between our ribs
thread with snags, thin like blood; what
we had was a rag or scrape, was run or fat.

What we had dug at the mud of us
with a rake, salted the hull of us like a sail,
hunted us like foxes among the black-eyed swans.
The heart becomes a notch on a belt worn loose.
It has a burn like touch and with the wonder
of the blessed. The fists of it silk at the arteries
of us. What aftermath sharks out from under
its reef. Barely eats. Barely starves.

The Punishment of One Is the Love Song of Another

At last, I have found my assassin. At last,
I have struck gold. When my past hissed
with cobras, you let me sleep. When
I was falling, you brought the ground closer
and made gravity of flowers like a kiss.

One body moving is a seduction. One body
is a practiced leap and a parachute
unsprung. Only the scalpel knows the passion
of blood. We soothe it with cold and sing it
to sleep. We leap at the chance to be blistered.

We listen and stiffen. We pivot and reap.
My rib cage could be a wasp nest built
of paper. My hand could be the slip of sand
across itself to slake the great unknown.
Snow coughs along the windows now
and listens differently to the pure. Snow
brocades like cotton. Prayers, like burdens, go.

What My Mother Wears

The cloth hearts of marionettes
like the teeth of sharks around
her neck. Dried seahorses for
decoration, belfries for a skirt.
She has only one petal left; no one
can decide if she loves me or not.
She is smothered in a liquid that
looks like blood, but when you
taste it, it is eau de toilette. From
the day we met, I have been her
baby clocking down through
time, the weedling she forgets.
Her attachment to me breaks down
once she kisses the crown of my head.

She wears the smirk of a newborn,
the target practice of the weak.
She wears sheepskin while it is still
on the sheep. Her barometer reads
low candor like a pressure in the mouth.
She disasters it out in the public restroom
and her memoir happens there
in the mirror, where she will not look.
She cooks vegetables to mush.
She lusts after transferrable guilt.
She pulls a velvet rope; the curtain
goes up. She can sing and dance.
She can laugh or cough. When asked
what's real, she bows out, by choice.

My Mother's Interiority

China cups shudder, brittle as fists;
breakfronts wire glass to wood.
The pious mood of each relic fits
the beckoning with which we lift

it out. The cabinet houses
cloisonné eggs, a bride and groom,
the lean of a globe, lopsided plate.
The grate through which we look

shines crystal to glaze, browns
monogrammed lace. The clock hand
of the tarnished spoon tilts
to degrees signaling evening;

its silver bowl clips our gaze.
The music box no longer plays,
though, wound, it will pluck
through its tines. The days

pose like heirlooms, the days
antique, and no one knows the weeks
have ended, the ladle has bent.
The gilt trim of the vase lip

mends a fracture and chink.
The woman who once held it
as the gold cooled wore a corset,
a pocket watch, a casket, a mask.

Job's Comfort

Once you were a god I could feel
enter the house from my room.
Once I knew to shut the door
when you returned. Once my muscles
tensed in anticipation of the moment
you came and rained your anger
down; my sister and I cringed.
We'd hear the car pull in, snap
the television off, and run. But
there was no escaping the key
in the lock, the door swung back,
the sound of your heels crossing
the floor. We were soft-bodied
in our shells. We hunched
quiet as the corners where we
crouched. We split up to decrease
the risk. We would sacrifice
ourselves for one another.
Except I remember the night
you pulled her from bed
and set her before our father
to accuse him. How she must have
stood in the living room while you
screamed, head down, fists
clenched, although I couldn't
see. I was huddled fearful in
my bed. All I could think was
I was glad it wasn't me.

Nkisi Nkondi

This striking figure, with its serenely rendered face and
violently pierced body, was made to contain and direct a
spirit in order to assist people in need.

—Art Institute of Chicago

Hunter of murderers, of liars, of thieves,
she loosens tongues, will not quench thirst.
Pierce her shoulders to make it start, scratch
her glass eyes blind as bone. Place inside

her chambers potent herbs, earth from graves,
a string or shell. Activate her to punish
or afflict. Estrange her and an ache will strike.
If a dead deer lies by the side of the road, she

is the weeks of decay before it's gone, grinning
jawbone dragged by wolves. Rest your head
in her lap to calm your nerves. Place your mouth
to her breast to let the dead go. Sew her name

into the lining of your coat. Close her eyelids
with a gentle thumb. She exhales until the wind
blasts shingles off a house. Scrape her with blades
to seal her power, slit her with knives to awaken

a vow. Way to call a lover. Way to cure
the moon. She is carved from mortar and
oxblood and wood. She is carved from water
as it falls. Be destroyed by her image

when telling a lie. Let each iron nail
denote an oath. Her heart mummified,
jewel in the chest. Her fist is a lantern
infested by dark. Her dowry is dust,

or blood on the lips. Read the entrails.
Swallow dirt. Unbottle the cyanide gloom.
The facets of this can be read like braille,
unmask your hands from the past's kid gloves.

The Narcissist's Parts of Speech

She keeps verbs in their bee box
until they all are queens. She keeps
words clean as the bowel of a sink.
Nouns frost over like statues, runners
before a race. Predicates recite
a dialect she has lived, echoed from
the past. Her reflections there act
differently from herself. Pronouns
frame each beaker as a window,
the pouring in a gaze. Once,
her adverbs were sewn of leather,
injected with shade, left for dead
among newborn elk and shelled
seeds. Once, she was planted like
a grain. Once, prepositions of her
mixed, volatile and deranged. She hears
the doors of neighbors open, hears
the whispering for what it is. Half accusation,
half confession. Half gossip, half laugh,
half reason. Conjunctions leave her
on a speeding train, stationless at last.

Jennifer Militello

Nkisi Nkondi

Nkisi contain magical substances that, depending upon the context, are used for protection or devastation. Carved wood human figures like this one hunt wrongdoers in matters of civil law.

—Dallas Museum of Art

When her heart stops and they crack its cage,
when they snap the breastbone, split its plate,

one can see the lungs lift, the blood drum,
the entropy of empires as they bloom.

Her hands cross over her chest, holding the diorama
of the soft days in, and she sorts her walled heart's

letter to us, sent intoxications. Sleets fall
and skip in the lane. Ages drain from her face,

and beneath the blossoms, the palpitations of her
elongate and sleep, a hard beat, a skipped beat.

Trained to sing in a language she can't speak,
as hunger plucks her voice, a fixed laceration

at the mouth. The ounces of her black open
like a landslide, tremor and breath. Feel the cogs

in her, the dented wheels. Collect them in a vase,
let them die on the sill. The amplification of her self

is a carriage drawn over cobblestone. Horse legs shift
their pistons. Horse breaths rise like wool. The pull

of revenge, the pull of revenge. Let blossoms collect
at the back of a coat, let the nearby bridge fade

to naught. She feels time, already bones, stir
in its cradle. She has a wild on which she cannot bite down,

even when the bullet is offered and the amputation
begins. She won't be saved. You can chain her

and she will bow her head. You can break her bones
and they will arc with rain. Great beasts freak and lie,

shut up in a god, miles from the rudder of the body.
She has a nest that expresses like a star.

My Mother Is the Wasp Egg Attached
to the Belly of the Tarantula

Soon to hatch. Soon to unlatch
and crawl inside. Soon to liquefy
and siphon the guts. It seems
too much, to start with the tissue
then gorge organs out. To be
buried with an insect, then turn it
to a corpse. Larva-suck until
the final molt. The more she
is flesh, the more he is husk.
But the venom does its work.
The spider is still. Eye twitch.
Limb twitch. Paralysis lair.

How she grows to gain
the most painful sting. Gains
coloring that declares her unfit
to eat: aposematic blue-black
with molasses-amber wings.
Takes flight to ignite another
round of this. She finds you
by the smell, flips you over, stabs
the soft joint of the leg. Lands
on you, probes your belly, seals
the chamber, closes the grave.
Leaves me unborn, voracious,
ready to wake.

The Pact

Mother, I have destroyed you. Forgive me as I am
destroyed. The submarine of you, mother, has, underwater,
shipped me off, has fired on me, is nuclear. Mother,
the gold tooth of me is stolen, the frayed cord of me
is broken, the scored record of me is frozen, the scratched
recording of me is full. Fire on my self pulled from
a pile of the wreckage, fire on my plumage-self
planned in advance. And decorated for the homecoming
and sheltered by the colors and the blending in with ending
and the touch of a Cyclops to the backs of wool. Clinging
to the belly of the sheep, I come home. Mother, my blood
is the blood sum of you and my father. I have no choice. I need
your rules. And now the tides come in and, like driftwood, I
drift, and like summits I rest and like the Eucharist I am blessed,
and like the lost reflection I am lit from below by what
appears to be light. I say my name and it ignites. I say my name
and it tires like a rower on a stolen ship or lags like
a haggard sail. I lost my veil, I lost my bed, I lost what I thought
had been said to you to make you understand. You, the shape
eating waterfowl with bare hands. Mother, your grand chandelier
of lies has so many eyes it sees like a spider or a fly in every
direction; it decides, goes for miles. What opens before you
is my smile. Empty as a room. Empty as a foot. Empty as a ruse.
Empty as a lung. Empty as a tongue that has not said. Empty
as a vein that has not bled. What am I, mother, but the undead
walking the way you want me to walk, the way you want me to
talk, up from the grave at your command. The zombie I am, covered
in soot. Soon I swoon and faint and fall. But that is not all. I am
the spoon you cook. I am the food you concoct. I am the line
you lost with the hook at the end, meant to sink into a mouth.
My cheek is set, my wretch is good, I am not what wooed you. I am
no good. This I know. I had to sew myself shut. For years, I was
the rut in the good old road. Do not trust the old, do not trust
the new, there is nothing to do and nothing can be done.

Jennifer Militello

The two were one, now they are two. I was born, I was new,
then I spoke, I was no good, I was me, I had flaws countless and
contagious as disease, not the least of which grew. I was me, I was
mine, I was not yours. I could not be you. Mother, you took from me
the drought and gave it meaning, you smacked the pout right off
my feeling, you kept stars lit on the ceiling so you could navigate
out from my room. It was noon when the sun set in you. I felt
the earth cool. I felt the fires lit so those of us who survived
could go on living. I felt the beasts arrive when night was confirmed.
You killed us off. You felt you'd earned it, the right to make us
into what fears and what crouches and what grows cold. I could not
grow older. I could not mature. I was sure there was nothing
left. What I felt in the end was the blow of yours
sent across the miles to find me where I lay spent
and desert-like in the heat. Keep me here. I serve
your needs. The edges of me, mother. I cannot be
until you let me recover. I cannot run to the subset
of another. You are too wise, you know what the constant light
means, you know what grows where and how to twist it
when the darkness meets it so that it can moss over and meld
into a growth that will melt it down. You fungi plus silk,
the lurch of me is trying to unlearn all the confusions of you.
Mother, mother, quite contrary, how does your deadliness
grow? With a tooth and a rack and a craw and a sack
and all the daughters caught in their rows.

Tough Love in a Vulgar Tongue

She is baker-legged, a bad bargain, bacon-fed,
user of the back door. She squints like a bag
of nails. She is an admiral of the narrow seas.

She is adrift, a spoil-sport, a mar-all, aground.
She often goes against the grain. She is angling
for farthings. She is full of emptiness, a fumbler,

funky, a fussock. What a gilflurt, what
a rum dubber. Gimlet-eyed with thingamabobs,
she squeaks in the gizzard, she steals goods

for sale. She is hunch-backed, humdrum,
hubcapped, impure. She would no sooner
hush the cull than murder the fellow.

She's a hussy, a hizzie, she's got the blue devils.
Loafing as a couple of inkle weavers. Like an owl
in an ivy bush, cesspool needing to be pumped.

A girl with two black eyes. Chattering like
a magpie, pulling off her boots. Who could know
what to do. She is a jingle brains, a jackhammer,

a Jason's fleece, is even left-handed. Pug-nosed,
pudding-sleeved, purse proud, puzzle-text. Pupil
monger, quail-pipe. Quacksalver. Queercove.

Rabbit catcher, ramshackle, rascal scouring the streets,
more brawn than brains. Timber toe, tickle pitcher,
tow row, nimble-tongued. Unlicked cub, unrigged,

untrussed. Whining, whiddler, whistle-belly, whipper-
snapper. Wise acre, wolf in the stomach, word pecker.
Zig-zag or zany. Zad only a mother could love.

Jennifer Militello

Dear Hiss:

your fingerprint at my hush. Lifted,
lost. Rawness lush. You are the way
seeds nest inside fruit or carry in the
belly of the bird. You are the pen across
the page. You are the hinge on a horse stall
opening wide or a window opened
after midnight by a thief.

Dear hiss:

conceive. You not of the tongue or the lips.
You of the palate or teeth. Slither along like
a snake or the waves' backhanded retreat.
You of the air escape. You of the rain in the
leaves. Disapproval. Whisper. Lisp. A currency
of exhalation or balloon mouth or tire leak.

Once my mother hissed at me to get me
to stop. Again and again. I was saying
the wrong thing. I was using the wrong fork.
My name loaded with a helium tank's
pressure and set out to set me straight.

Dear hiss:

too many flies on a corpse. Glaze
on a vase, crazed as ceiling plaster,
mirror of my most dissatisfied self,
quieter than a yelp, louder than a groan or
snuff, you are christening me in your bitter
waters. I eat of your flesh. It is
nourishment enough.

Dear hiss:

you are one-tenth outstretched, one-tenth
slept, one-tenth woken up. You are balanced
on a wire or balanced on a plank. You walk
forward like one condemned to death. The
noose around your neck. The platform
dropped from beneath your feet. The snap
at the end of your life.

Once my mother slapped at me, cornered me
by the stove, fueled the pilot light lit. In a fit
of anger backed me up, did not believe I was
sick. My name a blue flame through her burner
lips. My name a source of the burn.

Dear hiss:

you make me wait for what's to follow.
I swallow all I meant to say. I hold my
breath. Is a rattlesnake near. Is a bomb
falling through the air. Is a thread passing
through the eye of a needle. Is the bread
that was to rise falling flat. Is there a
trickle of water rivering down through
the compromised roof.

Dear hiss:

vertebrae of air counted one by one,
column on which to raise a bank, spine
with which to stand and walk, you sound
an alarm more molecule than light, you
strip a blossom of its petals;
its stamens bend, its branches rise:

Jennifer Militello

sound like a forest growing from seeds
sound like lightning fusing sand to glass
sound like a lasso settling around the neck
sound like nevertheless

Poem to the Word of My Name

Of a vowel's fat lip. Of a consonant's black eye.
Of an alchemy like a dirt path or a train track

or a carousel ride. Linked together with string
the tongue provides as it loosens and contracts

and makes contact with the teeth. An end
is almost in you. Also, a sniff. A hook with which

to gather space. A growl or snarl at your finish.
A single star in the sky above, calling three kings

to the place where you rest. Name of mine
people say in their sleep. Oil in the lamp

that never burns down. Catastrophe waiting
to begin. Inside me, your insect legs sing. Inside me,

your cellos resound. Your particles are reliquaries.
Your monasteries dust. You are full of pins

and needles, you are full of crimes I have yet
to commit. Hospital ruins in which pigeons nest,

abandoned asylums overgrown. I imagine my mother's
first furtive glance, how she saw your syllables there

in the book or heard them said behind the flex
of a hand. Perhaps as a whisper that gave birth to

the wail of this daughter. A canvas sail opened before
the wind of the ear. Now I am here. I wear your sound

like a skin. To me, it is inaudible. To me, it is
a fingertip or heart cell. Wrist bone, rib bone, or tail.

Jennifer Militello

My Mother Is in Antarctica

My mother is in Antarctica.
My mother is at the southernmost
continent where explorers have died
without their tents and dogs have
eaten one another for want of food.
Among penguins, on a ship built
for weather, on a ship built for shore.
My mother is in Antarctica, clean
in the race to the end of the world.

It is her heart. It is her heart. It is
the coldest place on earth. It is
a sample of ice core one million
years old. I can imagine her
at its edge, walking out,
with the brittleness in her fingers
and her nostrils seizing up.
My mother is in Antarctica where
nothing borders, nothing grows,
ten thousand miles from other land.

My mother is the dead silence
that happens when the barking ends
and all the ships have sailed. My mother
in her seal skins, my mother on
her supply sled, my mother not dead
like the others, feeding her dogs to
one another, feeding rations to her wolves.
Starving down to her bones in order to
uncover her shape at its most unloving,

a sharpness she knows has been inside,
but only now can know. My mother
with her glow of a skin made new
by raw wind, with ruddy cheeks and

chattering teeth. My mother is left
without even a beating heart and, inside
her, the continent is counting down.
The ghosts of explorers ghosting
her hand, and her breath turning to
mist and icicles in her husband's beard.

My mother is ice crack and glacier
abyss. I imagine her here, still
witnessing herself as there is a slow
freeze from her black heart onward
to the sled-pulling dogs, as there
is a small flame where she would
warm her hands, but her wool mittens
stiff with wet, but her trimmed hair
riven with ice, but her chapped
hands signaling and injured, but
the bulk of her body unseen beneath

layers and a scarf over her mouth
moistened as she speaks. As it
all freezes over, her eyes are shut,
flakes at her lashes, flakes at her
lips, and I imagine her ice queen
at last, crowned, jagged blackening
of her shadowed face, wind howling,
wind biting. Ice storm taking the shape
of her behaving as she always does before
all she endeavors to injure takes flight.

My mother is a continent
at the bottom of the earth. No one
can live near her. Men freeze for less.
Daughters are lain into coffins
at best. Marker of the planet's
magnetic field, farthest pole,
planted with flags, my mother lags
and withers with the mystery

Jennifer Militello

of the gods; she knows hard weather,
the cruel slow death, the long endeavor,
the journey for country or for self
across a vacant series of fields, across
the frostbite-wielding bluffs.
Softnesses erased. My mother is
in Antarctica: I can feel myself grow
older than the ice there at her feet.

I can feel myself flee yet again her
harsh climate. Dog at her sled, scarf
at her mouth, flake in her hair: my
inevitable melt. With an impermeable
seal closed over, of water at a temperature
where it must congeal. My mother
touching the explorer's ice pick bones
and stumbling on the corpses of men
and finding the preserved remains.

An ice river with the transparent blue
of frozen-over gone wrong. It will
be this way as tectonic plates scrape
at one another. It will be this way when
she sheds her layers and steps from
the ice and sails the long miles, away
from hardship, but not toward home.

Idolatry

My lover: butterfly on a pin. Sickness
in a church. Worship that will stick. Fuse
that will not filament. Grittiness
to burn. My lover is the knife edge
or half threat, the fire sip or godsend.
My lover is the hemlock I drop in the glass.
Facts I can't believe. Is a casino bet or
a dog year or an early death. On his knees,
like his mistress wants. On his knees, my master
wins. We reenact the stations of the cross.
We cry the way doves in mourning call.

I want to bite so deeply he bears a scar.
I want him to hurt, with me as the cause.
I want him to bleed secretly, silently,
like a bullet hole that only seems a bruise.
I want there to be no remedy or 911 call.
Do I want to kill him? I can't be sure.
But I want our small city preserved. I want
a Pompeii of bones I can show off. I want
destruction like a temple we can bury in ash.

I want terracotta warriors lined up. I want
mummies in chemicals lethal if sipped, scarabs
in the chest. I want x-rays to find out how
we were posed, what jars were filled, what water
we poured. Through his cheek, a worm or root.
Through his hands, a tar or frost. Through
his ribs, split by insects or weeds,
I remember the tender O of his mouth.

How Feeling Too Much Is Like Tracking or Taxidermy

If I keep my binoculars focused on
the past field, something might arrive
to coax the present field from its ghost.

Only the rude meadows snow.
Echoes die the way sheep lie down,
shorn and in melancholy groups.

I crouch small at the quick of the earth.
When I act, it is merely a catastrophe. I create
a fiction of my breath when I breathe out.

When the soon-footed print of a mammal comes,
the sound is like reeds as they knock at one another,
like measuring cups nesting in a drawer.

Wire me in a trap, but my tendrils will swell up.
As my lover springs from the minerals,
I spring from the fern-bitten dust.

In the Rainshadow of Whom

There has never been such a heart. The cost
of its gaunt priors rush. The lust of its far font.

The ease with which we pair and enlarge. And
bond and brunt, run and start. You are

my crowbar, my roll call, my choke chain;
you are my caudate nucleus. I am a cyborg

working spider legs and spinning from
my spinneret and spinning from my brain.

The past grows a crust. I burn a cage
out of the cage, where it captures like

honey, stiffens like glass. List and list and list
and list. I cannot be fed through the door's

shrunken slot. What is it want does.
The world gone sweet with the force

of the worm. Quelled keen from such a smudge
and rift, and racked there with the dapple of it.

Blooded Cold

The reptile house and its cool dark cannot outdark
your torso's void. You smart with my examination.
My hands snake and slither and clamp, snap a turtle's jaw
at your interior. Damp as a habitat, with a few bare shrubs

and shallow bowls soon to be filled, you cloud with being
what you would. You ruin with behaving as you can. You
practice the pathology of a trapped beast. In captivity, your
neck cranes toward the light. I put you on the laboratory tray

and let the too-bright brightness reproduce. Then I see the ribs
of you, and also the clavicle, and also the truth. The brightness
lit, then lit on through. Now I see the skins of you and they are
the skins of quarry you've tanned and worn, in place of your own,

when your own proved too thin, spotted or torn. You
made do, you tripped along, until you found you could
camouflage with layers of a sort. And so you were made. And so
you were born. I have found the ounces you wished to preserve

and the jewels mummified to your chest. I have found the abyss
you slip out in the night, through which you then return.
I photocopy to find your heart, your sorrow, your arms.
An extra organ or two. A healed bone. Jagged. Gone. Tusks

of ivory, teeth like prongs. I impale myself, I do. I found you
there, your outside shapes. I found you there, your inside god.
I have earned this. I have learned it. I will darn it. I will
wear it. I will knit you into the situations you never wanted to

admit to and make you rise on hind legs and make you take
a rider on your back and make you extend your sleeping limbs,
transform you from a creature of four appendages to two.
Until you are you again. Until you are near. Until you are new.

Jennifer Militello

How to Construct the Hero of a Western

Let the perishing take on a kind of art. Let
it outwit you. Saddle up. Steal the steed

and gallop out. Once I've been lassoed, you sever
the cord. We overpay. We lay me down. Our lines

are scuppered. The frame aslant. I touch your face
with its pinch and draw. I go the old way: the sky's

a yawn. You have a trigger-happy look. You point out
constellations and the spaces holstered between them

speak. Between them, we disagree. Your weathervane
points north when the wind is blowing south. The man

on horseback at the top is solitary. Made of rust.
You crush a little rock dust in your hand. You stand

with your profile in contrast to the fields. It heals me
to have to injure you. It's what I do to hold you close.

You want to kiss me. What do you think will happen
when you do? I tighten the cinch. I spur the boot.

If Our Love Were Jonestown

We would sign our Compromises, not knowing
what they say, and in this way pledge to stay,
and in this way create a cult for two. We would

give up all we want and are. Emptied syringes
surrounding buckets of drink. The unwilling
in us would be injected with poison,

or shot. The promise of joy would lead us.
There'd be a house at the head of the hive of houses
telling us what we thought. Children would emerge

from the jungle with jungle in their eyes, with
their eyes wide, and hands crusted with dirt.
Children would disappear into the jungle, their lips

stained. We would rest beneath the churned-up soil,
among the empty cigarette packs, among animal bones,
an arrow head, torn carpet and damaged tile.

Love would be twelve miles long and seven miles
wide, the size of something that could have been
real and turned out to be a lie. Our white nights

would be so white none of us would get out alive.
We'd endanger ourselves with what we believe,
with how we follow. What we feel is our leader,

and the real paranoia. All the drills will have us
thinking we'll live through it. But we won't in the end.
Now I know I can trust you, my darlings. Go now. Sleep tight.

Tight is how we'll sleep. Our breath in our chests. Nothing
let out. They'll come around with stethoscopes to be sure
we are dead. If not, we are shot. But *we* are them.

Jennifer Militello

We kill the children inside us first. And this is why
we die. We want to belong. We perfect believing. We
perfect trust. Until it kills the children. Until it kills us.

Lake Natron

—after Nick Brandt

Your love's thermal waters, kept from sun
for ten thousand years: others heal,

but I am the gilded head of Minerva found,
helmet axed free. Altars of the hair shirt,

pews of the split lip. Piranhas of salt,
my limbs soldered clean. Metal cleared

of its corrosion, garbage of its stink.
My joints stiffen, my legs refuse,

my lungs close over like notes
from a yew piano, its ebony keys.

Its wires weave my fingers as they fossilize
in place: strike them with hammers,

they resonate. Strike them with hammers
and they make a beauty that snails into the ear

even if you fail to listen. Capture me in any pose.
Coat me over and prop me up. You call it love,

but it is a glove at the face, a preservation
of shapes the museum desecrates. A blood-red lake

like your heart supposedly grown, but stunted
and bloodless and old. Calcium scours names

from graves, sulfur rises, minerals displace.
The limestone statues of my ankles eat away.

A City Mapped Out in Conversation

—after Lowry

Do not invoke the ghost of our separation.
The doldrums of our own malfunction.
The inside eye of bronze, our hollow
of corrosion, the brow, the nostril, the lips.
Do not clip from us the dirigible heart,
pierce it and squeeze out all the air;
it withers, only half inflates. I taste
the plaque, the Plimsoll line, the neckties
of its urban streets, its rivers turned
to mill wheels. Rivers, and their imprints
raw. Rivers, and their spinnings,
smoke. Do not draw their veils, do not
call the fever van along the handcuffed,
stagnant routes, bloodless footsteps,
hungers, grates, a woman's body pulled
from the canal. Do not drag the sky's
odd dark, bitter as brawls, fickle
as rain, sacks gone foul and mixed
with ash, ailing galleries, a braid of heights.
Do not leave the ghost unchanged. A church
or chimney, its filled motif, particled
and picturesque. Hands washed in waters
poisoned, clean. The skyline as a metaphor
for dusk. Fields of grasses long as graves.

Electric Fence

My collar is my lover's death.
I wear it heavy. I wear it
hellish as a home or shell,
hollow as a wreck. I wear it
well as he tells me he would
end, painless, as he lays
need like cobblestone, and
pressure like a sieve. I want
him to live, but we do not
fit. I want him to live,
but I writhe and twist and
an animal in me lies down
on its side and withers to bone
through our time-lapsed lips.
I want out, but out is not
bliss. Nor breath. Is a vice
or grip. I imagine him
taking pills and letting go,
farther than he's ever gone,
and how he would be missed.
My future rises up like gulls
drift on wind. My future
rises up like manhole cover
steam. My futures disappear.
One future remains and it
is by his side, in the chains
of his hand, it is by his side,
welded, tethered by all
he demands. It is by his side,
and in the crystal ball
he wields, all is healed, though
upside down. I say goodbye
to anyone else. I say goodbye
to myself. I give my limbs

Jennifer Militello

and give my steps to
give him life. His empty
eyes fill; he hinges, he stands.

Ode to Love

Place its toothpicked pit in water, watch the grist
of its insides grow. Witness its populous bloom,

honeycombed with rough. Its cobblestones grip
the heart in their mitt, a closed fist thickened

and gritty as silt. The swamp of the plumb beat
adamant as weeds. The dish of which is salted

by complexities or cries. It is a house in which
we cannot live, the quiver on an arrow

we cannot launch. It grows late over Nevada
as we watch. Strikes its gullies: we grow burnt

as a moth. Mimics a sleep of archives and
the small lies we forget. Mimics all laughter

broken by the time it leaves the mouth.
With its moving parts, its chimes, its gleam,

it muddies our archways, lying low, gives off
noise and steam; its mechanics clear the fence.

It must be wooed. Must be quieted. *Hush.* It must
be soothed. Has a snag. Has a bleed. A drape.

Flaps awkwardly at its edges, a heron.
At its center, a wide bottom perfect with fish.

Notes

"Agape Feast"
The Agape, or Love, Feast is a Christian fellowship meal recalling the meals
Jesus shared with disciples during his ministry.

"Geographic Tongue"
Geographic tongue is an inflammatory condition that takes its name from the
map-like appearance of the tongue. It is characterized by areas of smoothness
which migrate over time.

"Nkisi Nkondi"
The nkisi nkondi was a power figure of the Congo which acted as a physical
container for otherworldly spirits. The sculpture had the power to heal or
protect or punish wrongdoers, and was activated by hammering nails or blades
into its body.

"Tough Love in a Vulgar Tongue"
Much of the language in this poem was taken from *A Classical Dictionary of
the Vulgar Tongue,* by Captain Francis Grose, edited by Eric Partridge.

"If Our Love Were Jonestown"
Jim Jones ran the Jonestown cult in Guyana, famous for the mass suicide caused
by the ingesting of a poisoned drink. According to former member Teri Buford
O'Shea, Jones also had the members sign blank pieces of papers called Compro-
mises and later used them to blackmail members who wanted to leave. The cult
leader ran "suicide rehearsals" called White Nights, where the members drank
the drink but did not die. The italicized portion of the poem is a quote from
Jones, supposedly said over a loud speaker after the White Nights were over.

"Lake Natron"
Nick Brandt made a series of photographs of dead animals mummified by the
salts of Lake Natron in Tanzania.

"A City Mapped Out in Conversation"
This poem takes its inspiration from the exhibition *Lowry and the Painting of
Modern Life,* held June-October 2013 at the Tate Britain in London.

Acknowledgments

Grateful acknowledgment is made to the editors of the following journals, in which these poems first appeared:

Academy of American Poets Poem-a-Day: "Lineage Is Its Own Religion," "Ode to Love"

American Poetry Review: "&," "Chemistry," "Electric Fence," "Pledge," "The Pact"

Bennington Review: "Sibling Invention," "Sibling Parasitic"

Boston Review: "Odaxelagnia"

Connotation Press: "Dear Hiss:," "My Mother Is in Antarctica," "Poem to the Word of My Name," "Sibling Medusa," "What My Mother Wears"

Green Mountains Review: "Lake Natron," "Sibling Frankenstein," "The Narcissist's Parts of Speech"

The Iowa Review: "Erotomania," "Feeling Too Much Is Like Tracking or Taxidermy"

The Kenyon Review: "Nkisi Nkondi [Hunter of murderers, of liars, of thieves]," "Oxymoronic Love"

New England Review: "Agape Feast"

North American Review: "Geographic Tongue," "In the Rainshadow of Whom," "Ode to Superstition"

Pleiades: "My Mother's Interiority"

Poetry London: "A City Mapped Out in Conversation," "Fretwork," "Nkisi Nkondi [When her heart stops and they crack its cage]"

Southword (Ireland): "How to Construct the Hero of a Western"

Jennifer Militello

Tin House: "Job's Comfort"

Waxwing: "Homesickness Is a Geographic Nostalgia," "Species," "The Love Song of One Is the Punishment of Another"

West Branch: "Idolatry"

"The Punishment of One Is the Love Song of Another" appears in *Best American Poetry 2020*, edited by Paisley Rekdal and David Lehman.

"Job's Comfort," "Oxymoronic Love," and "The Pact" were reprinted by The Academy of American Poets at Poets.org.

"Nkisi Nkondi [Hunter of murderers, of liars, of thieves]"was reprinted in *City of Notions: An Anthology of Contemporary Boston Poems,* edited by Danielle Legros Georges.

Thank you also to Traci Brimhall, Jeffrey Levine, and Tim Liardet for their help in shaping this book.

Jennifer Militello